♦ ♦ ♦ ♦ ♦ ♦ ♦ ♦ ♦ ♦

A
DAY IN
YOUR
PRESENCE

♦ ♦ ♦ ♦ ♦ ♦ ♦ ♦ ♦ ♦ ♦

REKINDLING
THE INNER FIRE

◆ ◆ ◆ ◆ ◆ ◆ ◆ ◆ ◆ ◆ ◆ ◆

A DAY IN YOUR PRESENCE

◆

*A 40-Day Journey
in the Company of*

FRANCIS OF ASSISI

Devotional Readings Arranged by
David Hazard

BETHANY HOUSE PUBLISHERS
MINNEAPOLIS, MINNESOTA 55438

Copyright © 1992
David Hazard
All Rights Reserved

Published by Bethany House Publishers
A Ministry of Bethany Fellowship, Inc.
6820 Auto Club Road, Minneapolis, Minnesota 55438

ISBN 1–55661–206–0

Printed in the United States of America

To my mother,

Eleanor,

who is also a wonderful friend.

Thank you for teaching me the spiritual secret

Francis knew—

"Material possessions are not important."

Rekindling the Inner Fire Devotional Series

Foreword

*I*f you've never fallen in love—I mean head-over-heels and crazy-in-love—you'll never understand Francis of Assisi.

Francis was, above all, a born lover. Once he fixed his affections upon some object, he was abandoned to it body and soul.

In thirteenth-century Italy, a man like that was destined for greatness or for destruction—Italy, and all of Europe for that matter, was caught in political and spiritual maelstroms, driven by the excesses of madmen and heretics. Which is to say, it has always been easy to set the masses in motion with a lot of wind and noise. A true man or woman of God could be burned or beheaded, while the blood-lust of the tyrant ruled as often in church as in castle.

We are talking about an age of superstition and misbegotten visions. The children's crusades stand out painfully. So what was one more fevered visionary? Why would one man—Francis, the unspoiled son of a money-grubbing cloth merchant—burn so brightly?

On first look, it's easy to see that Francis stood

against the excesses of his age, including the spiritual. Instead of wealth, Francis chose poverty. Instead of superstition or mysticism, he fed on the Word of God.

But there was something greater. Francis caught sight of the One who is the heavenly lover—Love itself—calling him to follow. The eyes of his inner man were opened, and he began to walk after God.

What did he see? How did he follow? Can we find the path, too?

Before we commit ourselves to a devotional journey in the company of Francis, it's interesting to know how he blundered onto the spiritual path. For despite some unusual circumstances, Francis Bernardone was not "born" a saint. . . .

Many like to think of Francis of Assisi as the man who preached sweetly to birds and animals, and convinced a wolf to stop eating children. Some add to that image the firebrand reformer preaching the dangers of hell to a Church gone putrid in its own sinfulness. For those, a brief account of his early life may come as a shock.

In the fall or winter of 1181–82, in the Umbrian hill town of Assisi, north of Rome, a son was born to Pietro Bernardone and his delicate wife, Pica.

Pica was French, very cultured, and in her spirit ran a pure vein of spirituality. Pietro was a cloth merchant and would rather it were a vein of real gold ore. His every thought seemed calculated to advance his cash reserves and social status.

Pietro was away on business in that cold season

when the child came, and Pica called the child Giovanni in honor of John the Baptist. She sensed there was something different about this small one.

Near Christmas, a poor beggar came knocking and surprised Pica by delivering a prophecy. After receiving alms, the beggar suddenly lifted the newborn from Pica's arms and proclaimed that this little one would be "the best of all earthly sons of God." What must the young mother have thought, as she nervously rescued her baby from those filthy hands?

She herself was given to dreams and visions, but we know what Pietro thought of such spiritual talk: *worthless delirium*. Their son would also be a merchant. He would build the family fortune and perhaps buy his way into the noble class. Ignoring Pica's tears, he refused to call his son after some ancient lunatic holyman: The boy would be named Francesco, or Francis. Perhaps it would impress his finer customers that this child was a product of better breeding. From such details, we can guess why he proposed marriage to Pica. It's anybody's guess what she was thinking when she accepted.

And so, one struggle that would rage around Francis all his life—the fight between love of God and love of Mammon—began at the cradle. From childhood on, Francis was grossly indulged and spoiled.

Nor would the Church be of any help in reforming sinful young men. The spirituality of the early 1200s was rotten to its foundations. In Umbrian towns like Assisi, churches were often built on the fallen foundations of pagan temples. As if the ancient spirits still held sway—and likely they did—spiritual darkness strangled the churches. The Scriptures nested safely on pulpits, away from the common man, while weird superstitions governed everyday life. Instead of preaching against immorality, the clergy celebrated sex sins along with their parishioners.

What Francis saw, growing through boyhood into adolescence, was how swiftly the faithful could be "converted" to paganism. On a spring evening, youths on the village *piazza* could erupt in an obscene pagan dance. In its spell, they would weave through town, invade the church and lure the priests and nuns into the lewd parade, and all would end in some hedgerow or haymow.

You would think the parents were scandalized. Not a bit. Once a year, in place of Advent, the adults actually played a strange game with the children. From December 6 through Christmas, the villages were caught in a fever like a Roman "Saturnalia." Children took charge, and even elected a "boy bishop" to rule, setting off three weeks of gluttony and orgies. On December 26, to culminate these "celebrations," the real bishop submitted himself to the insults and degrading demands of the children.

To Francis' later shame—in fact, he damaged his eyes weeping over his sins—he became the ringleader. With Peitro's money pouring from his pockets, he bought the friendship of Assisi's young nobles. Wearing the finest imported silks, he led many a wild evening, and scandalized even sinful Assisi. Years after his death, written accounts of his early life would be burned by the Church.

It hardly mattered that Pope Innocent III viciously denounced these practices. The priests shrugged it off. *What was the harm?* The Church had already caved in to political power; now it was caving in to lust.

Then came Francis' bid for a place among the nobles. When Assisi declared war on neighboring Perugia, Pietro bought his son full armor—an expensive investment—and Francis proudly rode to battle among other "knights." He must have held his head high, watching the standards of Assisi's fine houses snapping proudly in the wind. But Assisi was squashed, and its young men thrown in Perugia's dungeon. Francis' health broke, and only Pietro's ransom brought him home, discouraged and beaten.

Had Francis understood how easily worldly wealth and strength could be ripped from his hands? We only know that a voice began calling to the spoiled clothier's son. The *farandole* was still tempting . . . but Francis was fast losing interest, and his friends couldn't understand. What was happening to their "king of youth"? Inwardly, he was searching for something higher, better, more noble. Pure.

It is Francis' inner vision that interests us now.

One day a beggar came asking for help "for the love of God." Francis drove him off—and was then overcome with grief that he'd driven God from his door. He ran down the road and filled the man's hands with gold.

Again, he believed he saw God in a leper. Fighting an urge to vomit, he kissed the man full on rotting lips.

Most famous is the moment when Francis fully denounced the world. Pietro didn't mind when his son squandered money on the young nobles—but "wasting" money on the poor made him violent. This piousness lunacy must stop. Possessed by a fury, he beat Francis with his fists. It's possible he drove his son into the arms of God.

From this moment, legend fights to take over.

Francis went to the village *piazza* and, with the bishop and the whole town present, took off his clothes and gave them back to Pietro. God would be his only father. In Hollywood's version, Francis left the village naked. In fact, he wore a hair shirt. The bishop draped his robe over Francis' shoulders, a sign, some like to claim, that the Church at once recognized this young saint.

But the Church had no clue what to do with Francis and his high ideals. He would live like the sparrow, trusting God for bread. He would wear rags not robes, sleep in ditches and cattle stalls. He was *in* the world, but no longer *of* the world. We would be wrong to fault Innocent III for being skeptical when Francis visited his palace in Rome, ask-

ing permission to preach. There was enough dis-
order, disease and poverty in Europe, not to
mention religious fanaticism: Did the Church really
need a brotherhood of beggars, trusting God *that*
completely?

Apparently, the common people thought so.
Young men began to leave castle and farm, donning
the coarse brown habit. They flocked after him
through the villages, while Francis sang like a trou-
badour. What was the message? Not just that we
should love God—and here we place a finger on
Francis' spiritual pulse—but *God is in love with us*!

"Nothing can separate us from the love of God,"
says the Apostle Paul. "Neither life, nor
death. . . ."

Having had all of the world, Francis would
prove one thing over and over: If just once you
catch sight of the love of God, you will know the
joy of living in His presence. And a single day in
God's presence, as the psalmist sings, is better than
gold.

There are many fascinating stories of Francis'
life that inspire and challenge. The Scriptures put
on flesh in this remarkable man. He could sing,
preach, or pray the Word of God at will. But he was
no limpid poet. His missionary zeal would take him
to Jerusalem, in the middle of a bloody crusade,
where he marched into the enemy camp to tell the
Sultan's nephew about the love of Christ. (For an
inspiring read, I recommend Julien Green's careful,
loving work, *God's Fool*.)

My hope is that *A Day in Your Presence*, like the other books in this series, will help you follow the pathways of Francis' heart. My suggested prayers are intended to help you make the journey your own, as I have. In the morning, may you learn to see the "sun of righteousness" rising to give you guidance and light. Through the day, may God's peace help you keep your choices simple. At night, consider how His loving care shines over us, constant as the stars, no matter our physical circumstances.

I've written my own response after each reading as a prayer. May the words of Francis, and the Word of God, set a new fire burning warmly in your soul.

David Hazard
January 1992

Contents

A
DAY IN
YOUR
PRESENCE

1
"I Give Myself to You"

*How great is the love the Father has lavished on us,
that we should be called children of God! And that is
what we are! . . . Everyone who has this hope in him
purifies himself, just as he is pure.*

1 John 3:1, 3

I am awed at the glory of it, amazed at the
great and holy gift that is ours—to have a Father
in heaven!

Deep within me the very wonder of it burns
with a holy fire. When I am faced with my own
evil, it warms me with consolation. When I face a
world of cruelty and vices, it brightens my soul
with its beauty and with flames of holy wonder.
To have a God who has willingly, lovingly
promised himself to us forever, so that He even
calls himself our spouse! (Jeremiah 3:14).

And here is another great gift I carry within—
a holy mystery, a wonderful thing that sets me

aflame with love, contentment, humbleness, peace, sweetness within, a desire to break open with love for all—a gift to be sought and desired above anything else (Matthew 13:45–46). To have a Lord who calls himself our brother, and our son! (Mark 3:33–35).

Here is the sealed proof of His love—that He laid down His life for us, His straying sheep (Isaiah 53:6; John 10:15).

This is the Lord who, with the compassion of a brother and son, prayed to the Father for us saying, "Holy Father, protect them by your name (John 17:11). I have revealed you, my Father, to those whom you gave me out of the world. They were yours and you gave them to me (v. 6). I gave them the words you gave me, and they accepted them. They knew with certainty that I came from you, and they believed you sent me (v. 8). I pray for them. I am not praying for the world (v. 9). Set them apart for your holy use (v. 17). For their sake, I have set myself apart for your use, that they too may be made holy (v. 19), that they may be one as we are one (v. 11).

"And I pray, Father, that where I am they also may be with me, so that they may see my glory (v. 24) as it shines into this world from your kingdom" (Matthew 20:21).

My Father, you welcome me into your presence . . . by the blood and the word of my Lord Jesus, your Son.

In this moment, in spirit, I want to be with you, sitting at your feet . . . enjoying your love . . . so that I may walk today in this thirsty and dark world and carry with me a cool drink of your presence . . . a reflection of your brightness.

2
Sing to Yourselves in Holy Songs

Be filled with the Spirit. . . . Sing and make music in your heart to the Lord, always giving thanks to God for everything, in the name of our Lord Jesus Christ . . . make the most of every opportunity, and do not be foolish.

Ephesians 5:18–20, 16–17

For the fool allows his heart to tell him, "There is no God."

Psalm 14:1 (paraphrase)

You are holy, Lord,
   you are the *only* God,
   and all your works are wondrous
   (Psalm 75:1–5).
You are strong,
   you are great,
   you are the Most High,

23

you are the almighty King!
You, my holy Father, are the King of heaven
and earth! (John 17:11; Matthew 11:25).
You are the mystery of Three in One,
the Lord God above all gods (Psalm 135:5).
You are good,
you are *all* good,
you are the highest good,
Lord of all, God of all,
ever-living,
and ever true (1 Thessalonians 1:9).
You are the fire of love itself,
you pour yourself out for us in charity—
You are our
wisdom
humility
patience (Psalm 70:5).
You are our
beauty
meekness
security (Psalm 30:5).
You are our
inner peace
and our joy.
You are Hope (1 Corinthians 13).
You are all that brings a sweet fragrance within,
and in you we are gathered into a life
that is eternal! (2 Corinthians 2:15).
Great and wonderful Lord!

You are almighty God who lives forever
and a merciful Savior who gave your life for
me! (Isaiah 60:15–16).

FROM A PERSONAL PARCHMENT

My Father, today I will shout down every doubtful and unbelieving voice within me.

I will sing and proclaim you from the depths of my being . . . until you yourself are my strength and my song!

3
You Are Always, Only Good

I heard the voice of many angels, numbering . . . ten thousand times ten thousand . . . encircling the throne. In a loud voice they sang. . . .
And I heard every living creature in heaven and on earth . . . singing: "To him who sits upon the throne, and to the Lamb, be praise and honor and glory and power, for ever and ever!"

Revelation 5:11–13

And Jesus said, "Why do you call me good?"

Luke 18:19

Let every living creature
   in heaven and on earth,
   in the sea, in the heights or depths,
   give praise

and glory, honor and blessing
    to Him
who suffered so much for us,
who has given so many good things,
and who continually pours out blessings
    forevermore.
God alone is our spiritual power,
    the very life and strength of our bodies.
He alone is good!
    He is the Most High!
    He is all-powerful, admirable, shining in
        glory!
He alone is utterly holy,
    worthy of our praise in all things, at all times,
    and in His presence is complete happiness
        today
    and throughout endless ages to come!

SECOND LETTER TO ALL THE FAITHFUL: 61–62

My Father, where there are living hells of thanklessness in me—of anger, accusation, disappointment with you—set me free!

Father, keep my feet from slipping again, so that I do not fall into the prison of calling you good only when things are going "my way."

4
Spirit, Open Our Eyes

Jesus says, "I have told you, no one can come to me unless the Father has enabled him."

John 6:65

I keep asking that the God of our Lord Jesus Christ, the glorious Father, may give you the Spirit of wisdom and revelation, so that you may know him better.

Ephesians 1:17

The Lord Jesus says to His disciples:

"I am the way and the truth and the life. No one comes to the Father except through me. . . . From now on you do know him, and have seen him" (John 14:6–7).

Philip says in reply to this:

"Lord, show us the Father and that will be enough for us" (v. 8).

29

Jesus answers:

"Don't you know me, Philip, even after I have been among you such a long time? Anyone who has seen me has seen the Father" (v. 9).

We understand Philip's confusion, you and I, because in truth God our Father lives in light which the flesh may not enter, nor even approach (1 Timothy 6:16). We know that God is Spirit (John 4:24), and that no one has ever seen God with human eyes (John 1:18). Therefore, God cannot be seen—unless one is seeing with inward eyes, by the Spirit of revelation.

Only the Spirit of God can reveal God to a mere man. As the Scripture says, "The Spirit gives life; the flesh counts for nothing" (John 6:63).

In the same way, since Jesus is equal to the Father, His spiritual presence and lordship over all cannot be seen by anyone, other than the one to whom the Father and the Holy Spirit choose to reveal Him (John 6:65).

All those who only saw the Lord Jesus according to His humanness—who refused to "see" and believe according to the Spirit and the Godhead that Jesus is the Son of God—these were condemned. . . .

Therefore, "do not let your hearts become hardened" (Psalm 95:8).

THE ADMONITIONS: 1, EXCERPT

*M*y Father, today I set aside all my
"imaginations" about you, knowing that human
imagination cannot conceive of anything beyond human
limits.

By your Spirit, quiet me now. . . . Come near me
in your bright love and holy purity.

5
We Stand Before You, Forgiven

I will be joyful in God my Savior!

———

Habakkuk 3:18

Your anger [against me] has been turned away, and you have comforted me. The Lord, the Lord is my strength! . . . With joy I will draw water from the wells of salvation!

———

Isaiah 12:1–3

The devil, that evil serpent, is most happy when he can ruin our joy; for the joy that comes from God is like an armor that surrounds and protects the very life of your spirit and mine (Zephaniah 3:17).

The Devil carries with him a poisonous grit, which he throws at us, and it settles over us like a cloud of dust, seeking to penetrate the smallest possible chink of our defense. This "grit" is

33

composed of doubts, accusations against us. If we are not on our guard, this grit will destroy the good, clear conscience God has granted us (1 John 1:7). It will soil the spotlessness of our thoughts toward God and others, and it will utterly ruin the pure-flaming brightness of our inner life.

But if we remain strong in spirit, the serpent scatters his deadly poison in vain. When we who are servants of Christ stand in the center of the Devil's cloud of doubt and accusation and instead of breathing this choking dust refresh ourselves in the water of God's joy until it overflows even in holy laughter—then not a single demon can harm us in any way.

But if you or I allow ourselves to sink under this cloud—becoming tearful, forlorn and downcast—we will be swallowed up in unholy sadness, which is not the same as the true sorrow that pricks when the Holy Spirit convinces us inwardly of sin (2 Corinthians 7:10–11). And it is equally wrong to go to the other extreme— seeking to escape heaviness and avoid spiritual struggle by losing ourselves in vain earthly enjoyments.

It is normal for a servant of God to become troubled in spirit. But when this happens, I do not allow myself to fall under Satan's accusing power. I stand before God, strong in prayer. I speak encouragingly to my spirit, insisting it stay in the presence of our sovereign Father until He floods me again with the joy of my salvation.

If we let our spirits linger under the Devil's cloud of grit, it will mount into a great billowing cloud of inner gloom, a heaviness and dread that will block the spirit when it tries to pray. And if this evil cloud is allowed to remain too long, it erodes our desire to seek God at all (Psalm 61: 1–2).

But God, who is patient and wise and good, will come to our assistance when we become cold and lifeless. And He will sometimes convict us of our true sin. We should be relieved about this, for then our heartfelt tears will flush out the Devil's mess. It will cleanse us in heart and restore our joy—which comes in knowing we may stand before God, in His light, forgiven.

THOMAS OF CELANO'S "SECOND LIFE OF FRANCIS"

My Father, you call me forgiven . . . free. And I hear you rejoice over me with holy laughter!

Have I missed something of what your Spirit has done for me?

6
Nothing Is Ours

The earth is the Lord's and everything in it, the world and all who live in it. . . . Who may ascend the hill of the Lord? Who may stand in his holy place? He who has clean hands and a pure heart, who does not lift up his soul to an idol. . . .

Psalm 24:1, 3–4

If your eyes are good, your whole body will be full of light. But if your eyes are bad, your whole body will be full of darkness. . . . No one can serve two masters.

Matthew 6:22–24

Great wisdom will come as you meditate upon this thought until you become firmly convinced of it: We own nothing.

The only things we should lay claim to are the sins that spring from our old nature, and every weakness of our flesh that would make us turn from following the Lord. But even laying claim to these faults is joyous to the true child of God, and not a morbid pastime. That is because we know the various fiery trials of life draw out of us all that is corrupt (1 Corinthians 3:11–15).

It is in times of spiritual trial that our faith is tested and refined. And when we go through times of suffering, whether in soul or body, or if we are afflicted by any evil person, we know that we are developing patient perseverance (James 1:2–3). All of these trials are part of the process by which our old life—all that mattered most to us—passes away, and we begin to walk in the eternal life of God.

Each of us must guard against pride and empty boasting, telling everyone about all that we own, and how much we know, and all that we have accomplished. And we must also beware of the natural wisdom, which is based upon the principles of this fleeting world (Isaiah 40:7–8).

A worldly spirit is easily recognized. It loves to talk a lot about spiritual things, but does nothing. It strives hard to be seen and esteemed by others as "spiritual," but lacks any desire for true piety, which comes only by growing in that secret interior relationship with the Lord who feeds the fire of real holiness (Matthew 6:5–7, 16–18).

This is the kind of person our Lord was referring to when He said, "I tell you the truth, they have received their reward in full" (Matthew 6:2).

The Spirit of God, on the other hand, continues to breathe His truth within us— whispering, beckoning, inspiring us to live the life of the Spirit. He always reminds us to consider as "dead" that lower nature which seeks life and honor from people. In fact, we should come to hate this nature, because it only leads us again and again into shame, into seeking our worth where there is no lasting worth.

You will clearly recognize the guiding voice of God's Spirit in this way: His constant aim is to lead us in paths that produce humility, patience, a simple life, and true peace in our heart.

And above all, He desires us to grow in deep respect for God. This we will do, as the Spirit helps us walk in the holy wisdom and love that come as we dwell daily with the Father, the Son and the Holy Spirit.

THE RULE OF 1221: 17

My Father, what great relief . . . that I can lay down the weight of self and look deeply into all that you are.

Lead me into quiet . . . into that holy place where you stand.

Fill my eyes with your light . . . as you guide me away from paths of tangle and turmoil . . . to still waters.

7
Rebirth

*F*lesh gives birth to flesh, but the Spirit
gives birth to spirit.

———

John 3:6, NIV

*C*ontinue to work out . . . your own salvation with
reverence and awe and trembling . . . for it is God
who is all the while at work in you—energizing and
creating in you the power and desire—both to will
and to work for his good pleasure. . . .

———

Philippians 2:12–13, Amplified

*B*e careful that you do not adopt the world's
manner when it comes to being "wise." The
world tells us we must be careful to see to our
own interests first, to plan all that we say and do
cautiously, so that in loving and giving to others
we do not give up anything that is "rightfully"
ours. May God forbid that we call this "wise,"
when it is nothing but worldly and selfish
calculation!

As God's sons and daughters, we should be without the kind of guile that gives to others only when it will mean a good return in some way for us. We should seek, before God, to be His humble servants, pure in our heart's desire to give and do, just as He directs us. . . .

God's Spirit will come to rest upon you, and upon anyone who will live this way, enduring to the last the constant temptation to live for yourself alone (Isaiah 11:2). The Father has promised that if we obey His command to love others, He and His Son, our Lord Jesus, will come and make their home with us and dwell with us forever (John 14:21–23). Moreover, we will be seen and known as children of the heavenly Father because it will be obvious to all that we are busily, faithfully doing His work and not seeking our own ends (Matthew 5:45).

When we live this way, it may be said that we are truly wedded to Him—in spirit, we become the brothers, the sisters, and the mothers of our Lord Jesus Christ (Matthew 12:48–50).

A man or woman begins to live in the Spirit by determining to become "the bride" of our Lord. In faith, we wed our souls to the Spirit of Christ and begin to enjoy doing His will. We become His "brothers and sisters" as we do the will of His Father who is in heaven. And we are "mothers" to Him when we allow Him to sit enthroned deep within our hearts by loving Him dearly and purely, keeping in good conscience by surrendering to His lordship over all that is ours.

As we knit ourselves with Him in this way, joined to Him in our hearts, a new spirit is born in us. Thus, our spiritual progress is similar to the way life grows within a physical womb. Eventually, we will no longer be living like men and women of the world. Instead, we will be so filled with the Spirit of Christ that we birth *Him* again into this world by doing the loving acts He himself would do if He were present in the body (John 14:12).

FIRST LETTER TO ALL THE FAITHFUL: 45–53

My Father, how can I thank you enough for humbling yourself so greatly, as to live within me?

Today, this is my heart's desire: that something more of you may be born into this world through me.

43

8
Our Position of Honor

Then Jesus said [to all of his followers], "If anyone would come after me, he must deny himself and take up his cross daily and follow me. For whoever wants to save his life will lose it, but whoever loses his life for me will save it.
What good is it for a man to gain the whole world, and yet lose or forfeit his very self?"

Luke 9:23–25

I want you to meditate on God's Word, so you will not become confused about the position of wondrous honor the Father has given to us.

It is true that He created our physical body in the image of His Son whom He loves so greatly, and He has formed our inward being in His own likeness—with capacities to know, to shape or create, to choose, and to love (Genesis 1:26).

Yes, we have been granted a place of high honor! Then why is it that so many lower

45

creatures serve and honor their Creator better than we do? For even the demons were not solely responsible for crucifying the Lord of Life—it was you and I who crucified Him, the power of our sin joining with them in this hideous act. And we continue to crucify Him whenever we seek life in sinful, corrupting pleasures that dishonor Him in every way.

Don't you begin to see what I am telling you? It is He who has chosen to graciously honor us. We have nothing to be proud of in ourselves.

Even if we knew all things—if we could speak in the tongues of men and angels so that even the very mysteries of heaven were like an open book—we could never boast that we deserved the position God has willed for us. (If the truth be told, even the devils know more about the workings of heaven and earth than the wisest Christian—so how could anyone boast, even if one were given a special revelation from God?)

Suppose you were the best-looking, or the wealthiest person on earth. Or suppose that you were so spiritual you could work wonders and drive out devils. Whether you are naming physical or spiritual strengths, what do you have that is not *apart* from you? What do you have that was not given to you?

What is left for us to boast about?

We may boast only in this way, like the apostle Paul:

"I will boast all the more gladly about my

weaknesses, so that Christ's power may rest on me . . . it is for Christ's sake I delight in weaknesses, in insults, in hardships, in persecutions, in difficulties. For when I am weak, then I am strong" (2 Corinthians 12:9–10).

Our "boast," our "honor" is in this: that every day our loving heavenly Father allows us to take up our cross and serve Him in the same simple obedience as that of our Lord Jesus Christ.

THE ADMONITIONS: 5

My Father, why do I try to conceal my weaknesses? Why do I so often pretend I am strong enough to handle life myself?

Uproot my self-sufficiency . . . my pride . . . and any selfish motive that keeps me from stepping out into difficult tasks you ask of me . . . for fear that I will fail.

9
Look to Your Good Shepherd

*I am the good shepherd. The good shepherd lays
down his life for the sheep.*

John 10:11

*Upon hearing [Jesus' teaching about laying down his
life in order to walk in the perfect will of the Father],
many of his disciples said, "This is a hard teaching.
Who can accept it?" . . . From this time, many of his
disciples turned back and no longer followed him.
Jesus asked the Twelve, "You do not want
to leave me, too, do you?"*

John 6:60, 66–67

*F*ix the eyes of your soul on the One who is
our good shepherd. He is the perfectly obedient
One, who endured terrible sufferings on the
cross to save His sheep.

The true sheep of our Lord are the ones who

continue to follow Him as He leads them through struggles, or mistreatment by others, or when He allows insults to be hurled, or through times of extreme dissatisfaction. They will continue with Him even when He leads through bodily illness, or spiritual temptation—enduring all things to the end (Romans 15:5–6). By walking with Him continually, they receive everlasting life from the Lord.

It is a great shame, to many of us who are known as servants of God, that while the apostles and early saints actually walked with Him through every kind of trial, we think we are deserving of heavenly glory and honor merely because we *know* their deeds from Scripture and can easily recount all that they said and did (James 1:22).

THE ADMONITIONS: 6

My Father, *is there someone you have been leading me to? A word you want me to speak? A simple and heaven-sent task you would like me to do?*

Help me to know *you in a new way . . . by your presence with me as I go and do what you command.*

10
Spiritual Meat and Drink

*Y*ou, yourselves, show that you are a letter from
Christ, delivered by us, not written with ink but with
the Spirit of the living God, not on tablets of stone but
on tablets of human hearts. . . .
[And it is He] who has qualified us . . . as ministers
and dispensers of the new covenant, not of the letter—
that is, the legally written code—but of the Spirit.
For the code of the Law kills, but the Holy Spirit
makes alive.

2 Corinthians 3:3, 6, Amplified

*T*he apostle Paul reminds us of a true word
we must never forget. The letter of the Law kills,
but the Spirit gives life.

There are several kinds of people who are
killed by the letter of the Law.

First, there are those who study and know
God's Word merely to be esteemed wiser than
others. Even worse, there are those who learn

51

God's Word so they can preach it in order to bring great riches to themselves from those who wrongly marvel at such preaching.

Then there are those who have no desire to follow the spirit of sacred Scripture themselves, but only want to know what the words say so they can command others to live up to them. These people especially like to give "wise" interpretations, which also cause others to marvel wrongly.

Then there are those to whom the spirit of the Scripture really does give life. These are the ones who know they can never in this life obtain a full knowledge of the depths of any scripture (Philippians 3:12–14), so they do not go about suggesting to others how "expert" they are in any given spiritual truth they have sought to learn.

Only in their words and actions will you know the ones in whom the spirit of God's Word dwells. For in their very lives, they will not draw attention to themselves, but will be like a clear glass through which you can see our most high Lord God, to whom every good belongs.

THE ADMONITIONS: 7

My Father, let me go deeper than words . . . so I will not be an empty, tinny noise.

I want to be clear glass . . . with only you seen through me.

11
"Love Your Enemies"

Jesus said . . . "I tell you: Love your enemies and pray for those who persecute you."

Matthew 5:44

*T*he person who wants to fulfill this command must learn the right way to love his enemy.

Very simply, you must learn not to be upset over an injury because it is an offense to you. Rather, out of your love for God, train your thoughts on the harm that your enemy is doing to his own soul with each sin or offense he commits.

Then it will become easier for you to show your love for this "enemy" by responding not out of anger but in godly kindness.

Nothing should upset the servant of God except sin. No matter how heinously another person may sin, if you allow yourself to become upset by the action and not because, in love, you see how he is damaging his soul, then you are just as guilty. Beware of storing up this kind of judgment against yourself! (Romans 2:5).

The servant of God who trains himself to live in this way—to become free from anger or upset at anything—lives and demonstrates a just life. He will become free from the oppression of trying to defend and protect anything as his own.

THE ADMONITIONS: 9, 11

My Father, take out my stony, self-protecting heart, which so quickly takes offense.

Let me love so much that I do not even see wrongs done to me. Let me feel only your grief for others when they fail.

12
God, Who Transforms Us

Without faith it is impossible to please God.

———

Hebrews 11:6

The angel said [to Mary],
"Nothing is impossible with God."

———

Luke 1:37

Almighty God,
  eternal, just and merciful One;
Grant us, who are in this lowly state,
  the power of grace,
  to do for you and you alone
  what we know you ask us to do.
Grant us always
  to passionately desire
  what pleases you! (Philippians 2:12–13).
In conforming our will to yours,
  we are cleansed in our inner being,

filled by your light within,
and our hearts are set aflame
by the bright blaze of the Holy Spirit!
This is the inner path we must walk,
    if we would follow in the footprints
    of your Son, our Lord Jesus Christ!
    (John 4:24).
It is by your wooing, empowering grace alone
    that people make their way to you—
    O Most High!
Yes, to you, who live and govern all things
in perfect Trinity, complete oneness,
    who are glorified,
    God all-powerful,
    forever and ever!

LETTER TO THE ORDER: 50–52

*My Father, I sense you walking close
to me . . . great and bright . . . calling me out of
darkness with a power that is beyond all I can think or
imagine.*

*Open my eyes, Father, to see that in me there is no
life, only darkness. . . . And to see all that is possible
by your grace, which makes me able.*

13
Wells of Peace Within

*Blessed are the peacemakers, for they
will be called sons of God.*

Matthew 5:9

*T*o be a true "peacemaker" you must work to
preserve inner peace, which will then govern
your mind and your actions. Do this for the love
of Christ, so that He may be seen in you no
matter what you suffer at the hands of the world.

A servant of God can never know how much
patience and humility is within as long as
everything goes well. It is in sudden testings that
our "treasure" is revealed.

When the time comes that those who should
treat you fairly do exactly the opposite—you have
only as much patience and humility as you see in
yourself in that moment, and no more.

THE ADMONITIONS: 15 & 13

My Father, if you had not assured me of your all-surrounding love, this would be a truth too hard to bear. And yet . . .

If you are with me today . . . in me . . . filling me . . . then when I am tried, your face will be seen in me.

With you I am ready to face this day!

14
A Whisper Between Friends

The Lord passed by, and a great strong wind rent the mountains and brake in pieces the rocks before the Lord; but the Lord was not in the wind . . . [nor] the earthquake . . . [nor] the fire: and after the fire [came] a still small voice. . . .

1 Kings 19:11–12, KJV

I have called you friends. . . . You did not choose me, but I chose you."

John 15:15–16

Remember at all times—it is God himself, breathing within, who woos us and calls us to live as His sons and daughters.

Remember His gentleness when you think of yourself as a lowly servant of the most high King. He is indeed King, but one who loves us as a heavenly Father. And when you gave yourself to

Him, you took within you the Holy Spirit as your spouse.

And so it is by the wooing, and the sustaining power of the Spirit that you chose, and continue to choose, a life of godly perfection that comes by walking the path of the gospel.

LETTER TO ST. CLARE AND HER SISTERHOOD, EXCERPT

My Father, you call me your child. . . . You call me beloved. . . .

I know that no service you ask of me today will be too hard. Nothing you ask of me will harm me . . . though you want to put to death in me the selfish . . . the fearful . . . and all that keeps me from walking close to you.

15
Jesus, Name Above All Names

You have deserted Me, your first love. . . .
Remember the heights from which you have fallen,
and return!

———

Revelation 2:4–5, Amplified

At the name of Jesus, every knee should bow, in
heaven and on earth and under the earth, and every
tongue confess that Jesus Christ is Lord, to the glory
of God the Father.

———

Philippians 2:10–11

Jesus is the One whom the Father sent to purchase our souls out of the prison of eternal death. He is the One who washes us in His most precious blood (Revelation 1:5).

We should still our hearts often, and think on all that He suffered for us, that at the mention of His name we are stirred to adoration.

Lay yourself before Him, in awe and holy fear and reverent worship. It is the name of our Lord Jesus Christ! Son of the Most High! Who is blessed for ever and ever (Luke 1:32; Romans 1:25).

Give praise to Him, for He is all good, and nothing but good dwells in Him (Psalm 135:1).

LETTER TO THE ORDER

My Father, how I do cherish your Son Jesus!

When I desert Him for other "lords," turn the eyes of my heart on the Man who went willingly to a cruel cross . . .

. . . out of love for me.

16
Clothe Yourselves With Christ

You . . . are controlled not by the sinful nature, but
by the Spirit, if the Spirit of God lives in you. . . .
Therefore, we have an obligation—but it is not to the
sinful nature, to live according to it. For if you live
according to the sinful nature you will die; but if by
[living and walking in] the Spirit you put to death the
misdeeds of the body, you will live . . . those who are
led by the Spirit of God are sons of God.
Clothe yourselves with the Lord Jesus Christ. . . .

Romans 8:9, 12–14; 13:14

Where there is God's love and wisdom,
there is no room for fear, or for ignorance.
Where there is patience and humility,
there is no anger, nor even irritation.
Where there is joy in being poor in spirit,
there is no secret covetousness toward others,
nor greed that leads to hateful actions.
Where there is peace, sown in times of
meditation,

there is no worry, nor dissipation of true
spiritual zeal.
Where there is awe and deep respect for the Lord
to guard the house,
the Enemy cannot get inside, or gain so much
as a foothold.
Where there is mercy in discerning the faults of
another,
there is neither allowance for destructive
excesses,
nor an unforgiving hard-heartedness toward
those who fail.

THE ADMONITIONS: 27

*My Father, what filthy rags of my own
"goodness" and "strength" am I still clinging to?*

*I pray that you will never allow me to "put on" a
spirituality that is only for show. Tear away the
graveclothes of my striving to look right for others.
Help me to recognize the dead person within . . .*

. . . whom only you can resurrect.

17
Peace Is a Window to God

Blessed are the poor in spirit, for theirs is the kingdom of heaven.

Matthew 5:3

Make every effort to live at peace with all men and to be holy; without holiness no one will see the Lord.

Hebrews 12:14

There are many servants of Christ who are given to prayer, doing good for the sake of others, fasting, and practicing self-denial so as to abstain from sin. And yet they miss the mark.

How quickly are you offended, scandalized and stirred to anger by a single word—all because you count it as a personal injury? How quickly are you offended when something you feel is yours is wrongfully denied you?

If you find this is true, then it simply means

you are not yet "poor in spirit," counting nothing as your own—neither reputation, nor position, nor possession.

When you are truly "poor in spirit," you will despise everything that causes you to be selfish and self-centered. Soon you will become so free in God that you take no notice of offenses, no matter how great or slight, so that someone might actually strike you on one cheek and you would not fail to respond in love (Luke 14:26; Matthew 5:39).

THE ADMONITIONS: 14

My Father, I've been looking for a peace that is the absence of conflict or irritation. . . . And now I see that my spirit is not "poor" as long as I keep saying "mine". . . .

Give me eyes to see through all worldly pressures that trouble me . . . to see into your kingdom . . . and understand your great, settled goodness toward me . . . no matter what.

18
Holy Presence

Jesus said . . . "I tell you the truth, unless you eat the flesh of the Son of Man and drink his blood, you have no life in you. . . . Whoever eats my flesh and drinks my blood remains in me, and I in him."

John 6:53, 56

Since we have confidence to enter the Most Holy Place by the blood of Jesus, by a new and living way opened for us through the curtain, that is, his body . . . let us draw near to God with a sincere heart. . . .

Hebrews 10:19–22

There is a great sin, which is the result of ignorance among many people, about the body and blood of our Lord Jesus Christ, and about His most holy, written words by which these elements are set apart for holy use.

We know that the bread cannot become for us the body of Christ unless it is consecrated by His Word, which opens our inner eyes to spiritual realities. For in this world, we have nothing and we can see nothing of the Most High God, or of the body of His Son in the fleshly sense. And yet He wants us spiritually to discern the sacrifice of His body and blood, and this happens through the words by which we have been made, and then redeemed from death to life (1 John 3:14).

Far from understanding such mysteries, many who minister the body and blood of our Lord sometimes do so carelessly. . . .

Are we not stirred within by a sense of holy awe, stirred to piety when we consider what is offered to us—that the Lord in His goodness offers himself into our hands, that we may handle Him and receive Him within our physical being? When we take spiritual matters so lightly, have we forgotten that we must also come into His hands? (Hebrews 10:31).

Let us quickly correct our wrong thinking about this and other deep spiritual matters. . . .

Whoever does not give the proper honor in such things, let him be warned: We are all bound to give an account before our Lord Jesus Christ on the day of judgment (Matthew 12:36).

A LETTER TO THE CLERGY, EXCERPT

My Father, how many spiritual realities do I miss because I see with the eyes of flesh, and fail to see with spiritual eyes?

Today, Father, let me see as you see.

19
Sweet and Holy Father

Find rest, O my Soul, in God alone; my hope comes from him. He alone is my rock and my salvation.

Psalm 62:5–6a

God alone is our salvation. Apart from the Lord, all is lost in darkness.

Day and night, our prayers rise to Him, and He hears even the deepest silent cry of our souls (Psalm 87:2). To think of it!—The Almighty one, the powerful Creator of all things, it is He and none other who bends low to listen tenderly to our cries! (v. 3).

This one who cares for me and you has also paid a great cost to purchase our souls from the dark kingdom of the Enemy. So why do we worry and fear, as if He will forget to save us from every enemy we must face in this world? (Psalm 68:19).

After all, it was God who drew me gently from my mother's womb. From my first day, before it was possible for me to know Him, He was the Hope of my life just as surely as I suckled life at my mother's breast. He is the giver of life, and my soul began to long for Him from the day I came forth into this world (Psalm 27:10).

From my first days, He has been my God before I strayed from Him, and had to return to Him in shame and disgrace. But He never departed from me, and never will He leave me! (Joshua 1:5).

. . . He hears my cries of confusion, but He is never confused. He has seen my disgrace, but He will crown me with honor (Psalm 8).

Among men, we may search for someone who can understand our heaviest griefs, but will find no one. We may long for a friend who can be always present, giving words that console and comfort, but we will look in vain (Psalm 69:18-20).

. . . He alone is our sweet holy Father! He is also king, God of the whole creation. And He stoops to listen . . . comes to our help (Psalm 44:4–8).

AN ANTIPHON FOR MATINS, EXCERPTS

My Father, you who know me completely; I will still myself now and rest in your arms. I know that you have heard my deepest cries . . .

even those most secret, coming from the silent places of
my heart.

Today, Father, I will quiet my soul's infant cries
. . . and wait with wonder for your help and salvation.

20
Our True Enemy

When I want to do good, evil is right there with me.
For in my inner being I delight in God's law; but I see
another law at work in the members of my body,
waging war against the law of my mind. . . . What a
wretched man I am! Who will rescue me
from this body of death?
Thanks be to God—[It has been done] through
Jesus Christ our Lord!
. . . through Christ Jesus the law of the Spirit of
life set me free. . . .

Romans 7:21–25; 8:2

*T*here are many people who, when they sin, actually believe it is the Enemy's doing, or that it is the fault of another person who wronged them and caused them to sin. Neither way of looking at sin is right.

Each one of us has a real "enemy," it is true, but this enemy is right within our grasp. I am referring to the flesh in which we live—the body, within which we first conceive of sin, and then

73

act upon our own sinful will.

Therefore, blessed is the servant of God (Matthew 24:46) who knows the true enemy—the selfish, fleshly nature—and who also knows that this enemy is able to be subdued (Galatians 5:13–18).

Knowing this, you must always hold this enemy captive, always guard yourself against it. As long as you do this, no other enemy, seen or unseen, will be able to harm you.

THE ADMONITIONS: 10

My Father, why do I think you will be so shocked if I let you see what I've done wrong? Why do I try to "cover it" from you, avoiding you as if you don't know every secret thing?

Thank you that you have set me totally free . . . without penalty.

Today, let me see this so fully that I stop blaming others . . . stop hiding from you . . . and simply say, "Thank you for your forgiveness."

21
Hold Nothing Back

What shall we say in response to this? . . . [God]
did not spare his own Son, but gave him up
for us all. . . .

———

Romans 8:31–32

And [Jesus] took bread, gave thanks and broke it,
and gave it to them, saying, "This is my body given
for you; do this in remembrance of me."

———

Luke 22:19

Let all people tremble,
   let the whole world shake
   and the heavens burst into praise,
when Christ, the Son of the ever-living God,
   is present on the altar,
   in the hands of a priest.
How are we to understand
   the sublime humility of this—

that the very Lord of the universe,
God and Son of God
    so humbles himself
    for our salvation? (Philippians 2:5–8).
Fix your eyes, my friends,
    on the humility of God
    and pour out your hearts
    in devotion to Him! (Psalm 61:8).
Humble yourselves,
    so that in due time
    God himself may lift you up (1 Peter 5:6).
I implore you,
    hold back nothing of yourself,
so that He who gives himself
    completely for you,
    may completely receive you
    (Matthew 10:32–33).

LETTER TO THE ORDER

*My Father, seeing that you have so
willingly, freely given your life for me . . . how can I
resist you?*

*This day, remembering all you have done for me, I
give myself—my thoughts, my words, and all I do—
into the gentle direction of your hands.*

22
Crossing From Death Into Life

The pharisees got together . . . and tested [Jesus] with this question: "Teacher, which is the greatest commandment in the Law?"
Jesus replied: "Love the Lord your God with all your heart and with all your soul and with all your mind. . . . And love your neighbor as yourself."

Matthew 22:34–37, 39

Jesus also said, "I tell you the truth, whoever hears my word and believes him who sent me has eternal life and will not be condemned; he has crossed over from death to life."

John 5:24

*T*he Lord spoke to our forefather Adam, saying:

"You are free to eat from any tree in the garden; but you must not eat from the tree of the knowledge of good and evil, for when you eat of it you will surely die" (Genesis 2:16).

Adam was given freedom to eat of every tree in that earthly paradise since it was not sin—as long as he did not go against this one word from the Lord. In light of the tremendous love and provision and blessing, disobedience in this one thing can be seen for the true evil it was!

Now here is the message that comes down to us, through our forefather's fall: We "eat of the tree of the knowledge of good and evil" when we take it upon ourselves to determine our own will. In so doing, we lift up ourselves—our desires, opinions and plans—above all the good things that the Lord would say and do through us.

Thus we must be conscious of two evil voices within. One is the whispering, suggestive voice of the Devil. The other is the voice of our own self-willed arguments as to why the Lord's commands are "too hard," and our many reasons why it will not harm us to transgress them.

Beware! When we obey either of these voices, and not the Word of the Lord, then what we "eat" becomes for us the fruit of the knowledge of good and evil.

Therefore, it is necessary for us to bear hardships, in order to subdue our fleshly nature.

THE ADMONITIONS: 2

*M*y Father, the only thing that loads a deadly burden on me is my own self-will, which so often keeps me in conflict and turmoil with you.

Forgive me, Father!

Help me walk again in a paradise of peace with you. I know I can trust completely in your good will. I can have confidence that nothing you ask will bring evil to me.

23
Guard Your Tongue

*If I speak in the tongues of men and of angels, but
have not love, I am only a resounding gong
or a clanging cymbal.*

1 Corinthians 13:1

*The tongue is . . . a fire, a world of evil among the
parts of the body. It corrupts the whole person, sets
the whole course of his life on fire, and is itself
set on fire by hell.*

James 3:5–6

You will become truly happy and at peace in
your spirit when you learn to love and respect
others as much when they are far from you as
when they are there in your presence.

Purpose in your heart that you will never say
anything behind someone's back that you could
not say (with God's love prevailing in *all* you do

say) when you are speaking with that person
face-to-face.

*My Father, before an evil word is on
my lips . . . stop me.*

*In this matter of my tongue, I know we have a good
bit of work to do. Rekindle in me a heart of praise, for
you and for others, so that only goodness is spoken
through me.*

24
Do Not Give the Devil a Foothold

In your anger do not sin . . . do not give the devil a foothold.

Ephesians 4:26–27

If your brother sins against you, go and show him his fault, just between the two of you . . . [and] if . . . your brother has something against you . . . go and be reconciled. . . . Settle matters quickly. . . .

Matthew 18:15; 5:23–25

Let all of us who are "brothers" in the faith take care, and not allow ourselves to remain in angry turmoil at the sin of another, or the evil done to us by another. Beware that the Devil would like nothing better than to use the sin of one to embitter and destroy many (Hebrews 12:15).

We must quickly remove bitterness in

ourselves toward any other, because we are instructed to see every fault of others through spiritual eyes, and to help restore the one who sins as best we can (Galatians 6:1). Our Lord himself reminds us that it is not the healthy who are in need of spiritual doctoring, but those who are sick (Matthew 9:12).

Through the love of the Holy Spirit, let us serve one another in this way.

THE EARLY RULE: 5, EXCERPT

My Father, I have allowed some bitter roots to remain in me. I have told myself it was better to conceal irritation . . . and anger.

Help me to see the truth, Father: Why do I let the bitter roots remain?

25
"Friends" Who Make Us Grow

*And we who . . . reflect the Lord's glory, are being
transformed into his likeness with ever-increasing
glory, which comes from the Lord,
who is the Spirit.*

2 Corinthians 3:18

*I offered my back to those who beat me, my cheeks to
those who pulled out my beard."*

Isaiah 50:6

*If someone strikes you on the right cheek, turn to him
the other also."*

Matthew 5:39

*P*ay careful attention to this teaching of our
Lord: "Love your enemies and pray for those who
persecute you, that you may be sons of your

Father in heaven" (Matthew 5:44).

For it is our Lord Jesus Christ in whose footsteps we must follow (1 Peter 2:21). Was He not being our great example when He called His betrayer "friend"? (Matthew 26:50). And also when He gave himself willingly to those who crucified Him? (Isaiah 53).

Whom are we to count as our "friends"? All those whose unjust actions and words cause us all manner of grief and trial. . . .

How can I suggest that you should greatly love such people? For this reason: Their evil actions draw out and display to us our own evil responses—anger, gossip, slander, hatred and the like. Then we see our sin for what it is. And only then can we repent and forsake it, and so we pass from death to the glory of eternal life if we wisely view our "friends."

THE EARLY RULE: 22

My Father, you have chosen all the people, all the circumstances that surround me. When I look steadily into the mirror of my life . . . at my own reflection there . . . I see so much that you are changing.

In your intense love, consume all that is darkness! Thank you for each of my "friends."

26
Father, Without End or Beginning

*For now we see through a glass, darkly, but then
[we shall see] face to face. . . .*

1 Corinthians 13:12, KJV

*Thus says the High and Lofty One who inhabits
eternity, whose name is Holy: "I dwell in the high and
holy place, with him who has a contrite and humble
spirit, to revive [his] spirit. . . ."*

Isaiah 57:15, NKJV

Lord God Almighty—
   holy, holy, holy One!
   Who is,
      and Who was,
      and Who is to come! (Revelation 4:8).
Let us praise Him,
   and give Him glory forever.
O Lord our God,

you are worthy to receive
 all praise,
 glory,
 honor,
 blessing. . . (v. 11).
Worthy is the Lamb who was slain
 to receive
 power,
 all divinity,
 wisdom and strength,
 honor and glory and blessing. . . (5:12).
Let us all bless the Father and the Son,
 with the Holy Spirit . . .
Bless the Lord,
 all you wondrous works of the Lord
 (Psalm 145:10).
Glory to the Father
 and to the Son,
 and to the Holy Spirit:
As it was in the beginning, is now,
 and will be forever!

PRAISE FOR ALL HOURS, EXCERPT

My Father, when I look to you for help and the window into your eternal real world seems darkly clouded . . . help me to remember your brightness!

By the Holy Spirit, cause me to rejoice, knowing

that I have come from a Father who is without
beginning and will return to a world without end—
and that for now I'm only passing through this tight
place in between, called time.

27
A Share in His Glory

*And the angel came in unto [Mary] and said, "Hail,
thou that art highly favored, the Lord is with thee:
blessed art thou among women."
And . . . she was troubled at his saying.*

Luke 1:28–29, KJV

*Father, just as you are in me and I am in you . . . I
have given them the glory that you gave me, that they
may be one as we are one.*

John 17:21–22

Hail, O Lady!
. . . Mary, you are the one
chosen by the most holy Father in heaven
    to be set apart for the holy purpose
    of bearing His most holy and beloved Son
    and to be filled with the Holy Spirit
    and so to carry the fullness of grace.

Hail to you who became His palace,
    His tabernacle,
    His home,
    who robed Him in flesh,
    servant to the Most High.
Hail to all the holy virtues,
    which are poured into the hearts of the
    faithful
through the grace and light of the Holy Spirit,
    so that from our dark and faithless state
    we may see the high goodness of God
and become faithful only to Him.

SALUTATION, EXCERPT

My Father, when I consider your graces—pure love, honesty and truth, peace that comes through resting in your will—I too want to be filled with all that comes through your Spirit.

What a wonderful mystery it is, that you want to share your glory with me! Today, make me like Mary, your "palace" and your servant. Let it be, Father, that only you will flow through me.

28
High Truths

A certain woman . . . when she had heard of Jesus,
came in the press behind, and touched his garment.
For she thought, "If I may touch but his clothes
I shall be whole."
. . . Jesus immediately [knew] in himself that virtue
had gone out of him.

Mark 5:25, 27, 30, KJV

*H*is divine power hath given unto us all things that
pertain unto life and godliness through the knowledge
of him that hath called us to glory
and virtue.

2 Peter 1:3, KJV

O most holy virtues,
    may the Lord protect all of you
    as you come down from Him to us. . . .
For each high truth of God
    destroys fleshly snares
    and hellish sins.

Pure, holy *wisdom*
    destroys Satan
    and all his confusing subtleties.
Pure, holy, *simplicity*
    destroys the "wisdom" of this world
    and the "wisdom" of the flesh.
Pure, holy *poverty*
    destroys the entangling desire for riches,
    jealousy, anger and hatred,
    and the cares of this world. . . .
Pure, holy *love*
    destroys
            pride. . . .

SALUTATION TO THE VIRTUES, EXCERPT

My Father, I cry to you . . . as
a newborn wanting milk . . . as a sick one needing
healing. . . . My goal is to take into me from your
deep, rich goodness.

Help me not to stop seeking you, drawing from
you, until my soul is satisfied with healing . . . and set
free.

29
A Home Within

The present city of Jerusalem . . . is in slavery with her children. But the Jerusalem that is above is free, and she is our mother. . . . Now you, brothers, like Isaac, are children of promise.

Galatians 4:25–26, 28

May he strengthen you with power through his Spirit in your inner being, so that Christ may dwell in your hearts through faith.

Ephesians 3:16–17

Let us make a home within our soul, a dwelling place for the Lord God Almighty—Father, Son and Holy Spirit.

We can do so in the following manner, as the Lord has instructed:

First, we must watch and pray so that we may escape the evils in this world, and which lead to judgment in the world to come. As we do this, we stand safe and secure in the Son of Man who has come to dwell with us (Luke 21:36).

Then, when you pray, fill your heart with this thought: "Our Father, who art in heaven . . ." (Matthew 6:9). Love Him deeply, reverently, completely, so that your heart becomes pure in Him. Pray always in this way, so that you do not lose your heart back to the world (Luke 18:1). For the Father is actively seeking those who will worship Him like this—remember, God is Spirit, and those who worship Him must worship in spirit and in truth (John 4:23–24).

And whenever you have a grievance, do not be led astray. Seek your help and recourse from Him who is the Shepherd and Guardian of our souls (1 Peter 2:25). He says, "I am the good shepherd who feeds my sheep, and I lay down my life for my sheep" (John 10:14–15).

Keep this in mind: All of you are brothers. . . .

THE EARLY RULE: 12

My Father, so often, I am not comfortable "at home" with myself. Or I am unsettled with those whom you call your children.

Help me to rest, Lord, and be "at home" with you. Come into all the rooms within me where there has been irritation, impatience, accusation.

Cleanse me from within. Wash me in your love . . . forgiveness and peace.

30
Who We Are Before God

When Jesus was baptized . . . a voice came from heaven: "You are my Son, whom I love; with you I am well pleased."

Luke 3:21–22

The God and Father of our Lord Jesus Christ . . . has made us accepted in the beloved.

Ephesians 1:3, 6, NKJV

In [Jesus] we . . . become the righteousness of God.

2 Corinthians 5:21

The servant of God who wants to live a life filled with unshakable heavenly joy will learn this: We must esteem ourselves no better when we are praised by others than when they contemptuously treat us as worthless and simple-minded.

All that matters is the mind and attitude that God our Father holds toward us. So what a man is as he stands before God, that he is and nothing more.

Great sorrow will come to the spiritual person who is placed in a position of leadership, honor and respect by others, and cannot see the distinction between the honor of the position and himself. And so, when the work that goes with that office is done, he will not "step down" and be a humble servant among the rest of his brothers.

And great joy will come to the servant who does not work hard to have himself placed in a high position, but always considers it an honor to be at the feet of others (Matthew 24:46).

THE ADMONITIONS: 19

My Father, *help me to cease my endless efforts to find honor and respect in the eyes of others . . . knowing that in your eyes I am accepted . . . righteous . . . well-loved.*

31
Sing a New Song

Do not love the world or anything in the world. . . .

1 John 2:15

You owe me your very self.

Philemon 1:19

Sing a new song to Him—
  sing to the Lord, all the earth! (Psalm 95:1).
For the Lord is great,
  He is worthy of all praise.
  He inspires us with awe,
    for all that He is and does
    is far beyond all lesser gods (Psalm 95:4).
Give to the Lord—
  every family, and all nations—
  give to the Lord
  glory and praise!
Give Him *all* the glory
  that is due His marvelous name!
  (Psalm 95:7–8).

To do this
    is to offer your bodies,
    and to take up His cross for you,
    and to follow His most holy commands,
        from now until the end (Luke 14:27;
            1 Peter 2:21).

PSALM FOR THE NATIVITY, EXCERPT

My Father, I see it now: when I am "singing" my own praises, hungering for praise from others, I am caught in the trap of self.

But today. . . .

Today I set my self *aside. Forgetting me, I sing a new song . . . words of love . . . sung only to you.*

32
The Fruit of Repentance

Be transformed by the renewing of your mind. . . .
Do not think of yourself more highly than you
ought. . . . Live in harmony with one another. Do not
be proud. . . . Do not be conceited. Do not repay
anyone evil for evil. . . . If it is possible, as far as it
depends on you, live at peace with everyone. Do not
take revenge. . . .

Romans 12:2–3, 16–19

*P*roduce the kind of fruit that shows you are truly repentant (Luke 3:8). Have you forgotten that our lives are short, and soon we will all stand before God? (1 Peter 4:5).

Confess all of your sins—which is to say, do not try to justify your actions, and stop blaming others for wrongs you commit.

You will be filled with perfect contentment when you do penance—that is, when you learn to repay others, quickly and simply, for the wrong you have done them (Matthew 5:23–24). For in so doing, you enter into the kingdom of heaven.

But woe to you if you refuse to repay when you have done evil to someone. For then you remain under the dominion of the Devil, for it was his evil work you were doing when you harmed your brother. And so you are in danger of eternal fire (Matthew 5:21–22; 18:8).

Therefore I tell you, beware of every evil thought. Do not let evil thoughts take hold of you, causing you to commit sin (Romans 12:1–2).

Instead, persevere in thinking and doing good, until the end.

PRAISE AND EXHORTATION FOR ALL THE BROTHERS,
EXCERPT

My Father, I stand before you, my merciful Father and Judge, and willingly acknowledge that my sin is my own—I blame no one else.

I thank you that the blood of Jesus Christ was poured out . . . and now covers my sin.

And I listen, obedient, for your word: Is there one I must repay? One whose anger or hurt I must willingly bear, in seeking forgiveness? Be my Helper. . . .

33
Hidden in My Heart

I seek you with all my heart; do not let me stray from your commands. I have hidden your word in my heart. . . .

Psalm 119:10–11

Be careful not to do your acts of righteousness before men, to be seen by them. . . . When you pray, do not . . . [stand] on the street corners, to be seen by men. . . . When you fast, do not look somber . . . to show men [you] are fasting. [Do all these things, only to be seen by] your Father who is unseen; and your Father, who sees what is done in secret, will reward you.

Matthew 6:1, 5, 16, 18

You will find yourself filled with heavenly joy and peace when you learn to store up in heaven the good things the Lord reveals to you (Matthew 6:19–21).

For how often do we speak a word of truth, secretly hoping in our heart that the hearer will think, "How deeply spiritual he is"?

The Most High will make himself known— whenever He wishes, to whomever He pleases— through our deeds. Or can we not trust in Him to accomplish this?

Therefore, blessed is the servant who keeps the secrets of the Lord in his heart (Luke 2:19, 51).

[In light of this], let us wisely consider what we say to others—how much we should say, and whether it is the most profitable time to say it.

Woe to us when we do not . . . let the good truths the Lord has set in our heart be revealed to others by our deeds, which would give glory to our Lord. Rather, we too often make such good things known only by our words, which brings glory to us.

Such "glory" is fleeting indeed, a poor reward (Matthew 6:2, 16). And those who hear our words, without actions, quickly lose what they have heard, and carry away little fruit.

THE ADMONITIONS: 28, 21, EXCERPT

My Father, what task of love can I accomplish for you . . . in secret . . . today?

34
His Reflection, Not Ours

Jesus said, "The reason my Father loves me is that I lay down my life. . . . No one takes it from me, but I lay it down of my own accord. . . ."
Many . . . said, "He is demon-possessed and raving mad. Why listen to him?"

John 10:17–18, 20

But we Christians . . . can be mirrors that brightly reflect the glory of the Lord. And as the Spirit of the Lord works within us, we become more and more like him.

2 Corinthians 3:18, TLB

*P*ure, holy *obedience*
    destroys every wrong wish of the body,
    sets us free from the deadly "works of the
    flesh"
        and binds us to the Holy Spirit

and to our brothers . . .
The one who possesses obedience . . .
   sees that whatever comes,
      whatever is done to him . . .
  is given from above,
     by the Lord. . . .

Salutation of the Virtues, excerpt

My Father, no one takes my life from me. . . .

That means no insult may steal my dignity, no imposition may steal my time.

All that I have is yours . . . at your disposal today. . . .

Be strong in me!

35
Ring Out With Joy

Behold, what manner of love the Father hath bestowed upon us. . . !

1 John 3:1, KJV

This is how God showed his love among us: He sent his one and only Son into the world that we might live through him.

1 John 4:9

Let your soul ring out with joy
    to God our help!
Shout, with cries of gladness
    to the Lord God, living and true!
For the Lord,
    the Most High,
    is the great king over all the earth
    (Psalm 47:2–3).
He is our most holy Father, in heaven,
    and He is our King before all ages
    (Psalm 74:12).

And He sent us His beloved Son, from on high,
    to be clothed in our flesh,
    born of the virgin, Mary. . . .
On that day,
    the Lord sent the gift of His mercy,
    and at night His song—
an infant's cry—
    was heard. . . .
The most holy and blessed Child
    was given to us!
    He was born for us! (Isaiah 9:6).
And though there was no room for Him
    in the inn,
    yet He came to be born,
    and was placed in a poor manger . . .
    (Luke 2:7).
Let all the heavens be glad!
    Let the earth rejoice!
    Let the sea and all that is in it
        be moved at such a wondrous gift!
    Let the fields and everything in them
        be joyful for what God has done!
        (Psalm 96:11–12).

PSALM FOR THE NATIVITY, EXCERPT

My Father, *when my soul wants to*
swallow me in its dark selfishness . . . when I forget all

you have done and look only at what you seem to have
left undone . . . forgive me.

    Open my eyes of faith, again, to your great, good,
unfailing gift of love itself . . . the Bread of Life,
newfallen from heaven for me every morning!

36
Inner Fire

He makes . . . *his servants flames of fire.*

Hebrews 1:7

Let your light shine before men, that they may see your good deeds and praise your Father in heaven.

Matthew 5:16

*W*e should all "preach," but do so by our deeds.

Therefore, in the love of God—whether you actually do preach, or pray, or do works in secret, whether clergy or laity—I beg all of you: Strive to be humble in all you do.

Take this as a warning: Do not allow yourself to take pride in anything you *have*, in anything you *are*, or in anything you *do*. If you become "puffed up" inwardly about good works, you will push right out of yourself the knowledge that, in fact, God has first had to do a work *in* you, so that He may occasionally do or say anything *through* you.

If you remember this at all times, you will be in keeping with what the Lord says: "Do not rejoice, even if the spirits submit to you, but rejoice that your names are written in heaven" (Luke 10:20).

. . . Seek holiness in the inner being, in the depths of your spirit. . . .

THE EARLY RULE: 17

My Father, thank you for writing my name, with your own hand, in the Book of Life!

Help me to keep you before me . . . bright-burning, pure and clear . . . as my highest vision . . . my best reward.

37

The World Behind, the Cross Before

I write to you, dear children, because your sins have been forgiven on account of his name. . . . I write to you, young men, because you are strong, and the word of God lives in you, and you have overcome the evil one. The world and its desires pass away, but the man who does the will of God lives forever.

1 John 2:12, 14, 17

The gospel . . . is the power of God unto salvation to every one that believeth. . . .

Romans 1:16, KJV

Now that we have made our decision—*to leave the world behind*—we have nothing else to do but simply follow the will of our Lord. As we do this, day by day, we will live lives that please Him.

Let us take care that our souls not become like

113

the soil along the path, or among the rocks, or among the thorns—as the Lord warned us in the gospel.

For the seed that fell along the path and was trampled under foot represents those who hear the Word but do not bother to meditate on it until they understand and it gives real light within (Luke 8:5). Immediately, the Devil comes and snatches away the Word of Life God has planted in their hearts. In so doing, the evil one keeps the Word of God from working actively within, which is how salvation is accomplished in us (Luke 8:12).

But the seed sown on good soil speaks of those who hear the Word, take it into their hearts to let it work. They keep in sight the noble goal of letting God's Word transform them into the image of their Father in heaven. So they meditate on it until it brings understanding—showing them their shortcomings and weaknesses (Matthew 13:23).

Their hearts are not "hard"—they do not deny their sin, or refuse to face it—rather, their hearts are "good soil." By patiently letting the Word of God work within, they cultivate the good fruit that shows they are growing in salvation (Luke 8:15).

We should do as the Lord says, unlike those who make excuses for their unwillingness to follow Him (Matthew 8:22). I tell you—be careful about this! For our malicious and subtle adversary, Satan, wants to keep every one of us from forsaking our sin, which allows us to lift our heart and mind to God. . . .

Let us always be on guard!

THE EARLY RULE: 22

My Father, help me to remember . . . when I refuse to admit I am wrong, then evil tries to grip me to itself, and slowly blinds me to the free life in you.

I want to keep your cross before me . . . and look beyond your cross, higher still, to see the glory I will share at your side.

38
In Your Company Forever

*Jesus looked toward heaven and prayed: "Father . . . I
have revealed your name to those whom you gave me
out of the world."*

———

John 17:1, 6

*One of [Jesus'] disciples said to him,
"Lord, teach us to pray."*

He said to them, "When you pray, say: 'Father'. . . ."

———

Luke 11:1–2

Our Father . . .
Most holy Father—
our Creator, Redeemer,
our Consoler, and Savior (Isaiah 43:3).
Who art in heaven . . .
You are in the angels and in the saints,
filling them with the light of love,
because you, Lord, are light
(1 John 1:5),

117

Inflaming them to love,
   because you, Lord, are love (1 John 4:8).
Dwelling in them, flooding
   them with happiness
because you, Lord, are the highest good,
   the eternal good,
   from whom all good comes,
   without whom there is no good at all.
Hallowed be thy name . . .
   May our knowledge of you become
      pure and clear,
   that we may understand
      how wide are your blessings,
      how long are your promises,
         how high is your majesty,
         and how deep are your judgments!
May your kingdom come . . .
   Govern our lives through your grace,
   and help us to come into your kingdom daily,
      with an unclouded vision of you,
      a love for you that is perfect,
         happy to be your companion,
         enjoying you today and forever. . . .

PRAYER INSPIRED BY THE LORD'S PRAYER

My Father, I praise you! I humbly
thank you for welcoming me as your friend.
   And for letting me know you by the name . . .
Father.

39
Lord of My Life, Now and Forever

*Lord, you have been our dwelling place throughout
all generations. Before the mountains were born or
you brought forth the earth . . . from everlasting to
everlasting you are God! . . . Teach us to number our
days aright, that we may gain a heart of wisdom.*

Psalm 90:1–2, 12

*Set your minds on things above, not on earthly
things. For you [have already] died, and your life is
now hidden with Christ in God.
When Christ, who is your life, appears, then you also
will appear with him in glory!*

Colossians 3:2–4

*B*lessed are those
who endure to the end,
for by you, Most High Father,
they shall be crowned! (James 1:12).

Praised are you, my Lord,
   through our Sister Death,
   who dwells even now within our bodies,
   and whose final loving embrace
   no one may avoid (Psalm 90:10).
There will be great sorrow and anguish
   for those who die in mortal sin.
But full of joy are those
   found to be in your will at their death.
   For the second death cannot harm them
   (Revelation 20:6).
Therefore, I will praise you, my Lord!
   I will bless you and give you thanks
      in all things,
   I will serve you in humility.

CANTICLE OF THE SUN, EXCERPT

My Father, you are the beginning and the end of my journey. You promise to go with me all the way.

One day I will step through a door called death . . . simply . . . easily . . . into your presence.

Today, let me come one step closer . . . in your Spirit . . . drawing my life within from you alone!

40
The Hymn of All Creation

The eyes of all look to you, Father of all, and you give them all they need at the proper time. You open your hand and satisfy the desires of every living thing. The Lord is faithful to all his promises and loving toward all he has made.

Psalm 145:15–16, 13

Most High, all-powerful and good Father,
    to you belong all praises,
        all glory, honor and blessing!
        (Revelation 4:9, 11).
    To you alone do they belong,
        for no mere man is worthy
            to mention your name.
Praised are you, my Lord,
    through all your creation
        —especially Brother Sun.
            He is the day,
            and through him you give us light.

He is beautiful and radiant with great
   splendor
   and so he bears a likeness of you,
      Most High One! (Psalm 19:4–6).
Praised are you, my Lord,
   through Sister Moon, and all the stars.
      There in the heavens, you formed them,
      clear-shining, precious and lovely!
      (Daniel 12:3).
Praised are you, my Lord,
   through Brother Wind,
      and through the air, so cloudy and serene,
      and through every kind of weather,
   through which you sustain all your creatures
   (Isaiah 55:10–11).
Praised are you, my Lord,
   through Sister Water,
      so simple, useful, humble,
         precious, chaste
         (Revelation 22:1–2).
Praised are you, my Lord,
   through Brother Fire,
      for he is beautiful, playful, robust
      and, like you, he is strong
      (Hebrews 12:29).

CANTICLE OF THE SUN, EXCERPT

*My Father, thank you for the gift of
this life . . . full of wonders . . . full of people I can
love for your sake.*

Thank you that I am surrounded above and below, behind and before, by you.

Today and all days . . . let me fix my eyes upon you . . . so that I may be filled with the inner fire of your presence!

DAVID HAZARD developed the "Rekindling the Inner Fire" devotional series to encourage others to keep the "heart" of their faith alive and afire with love for God. He also feels a special need to help Christians of today to "meet" men and women of the past whose experience of God belongs to the whole Church, for all the ages.

Hazard is an award-winning writer, the author of books for both adults and children, with international bestsellers among his many titles. He lives in northern Virginia with his wife, MaryLynne, and three children: Aaron, Joel, and Sarah Beth.